Third Position
for the Viola

book one

by Cassia Harvey

CHP214

©2012 by C. Harvey Publications All Rights Reserved.

www.charveypublications.com - print books
www.learnstrings.com - PDF downloadable books
www.harveystringarrangements.com - chamber music

Third Position for the Viola, Book One

Cassia Harvey

First Shifting on the D string

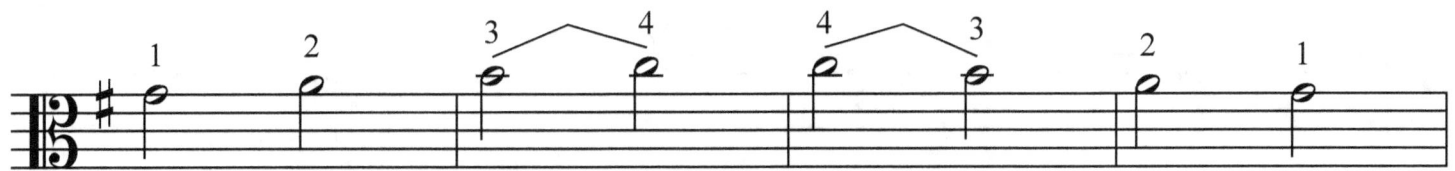

First Shifting on the A string

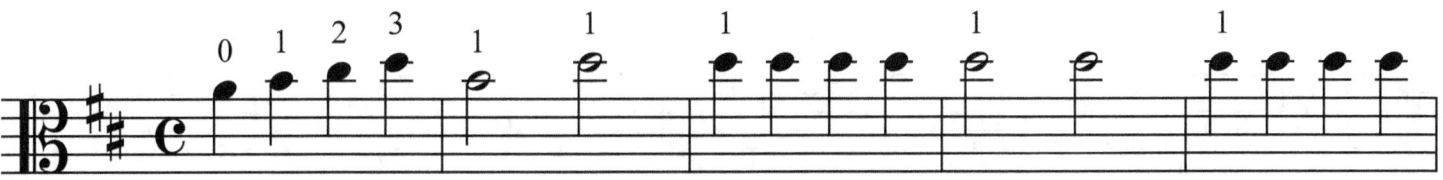

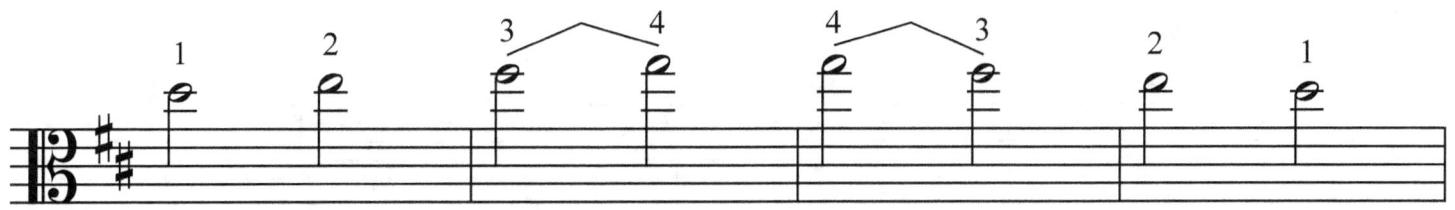

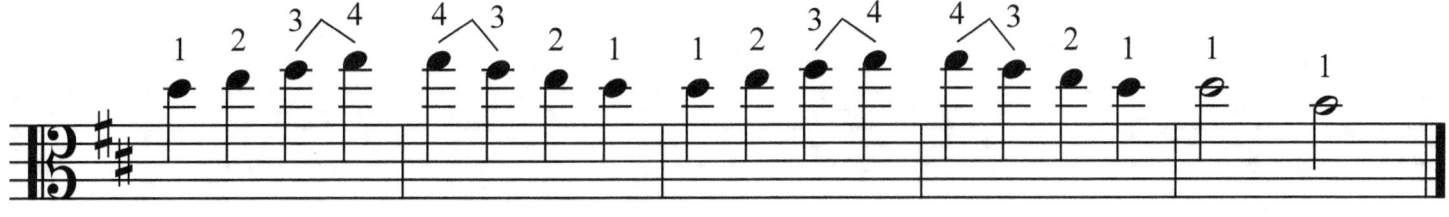

©2012 C. Harvey Publications All Rights Reserved.

First Shifting on the G string

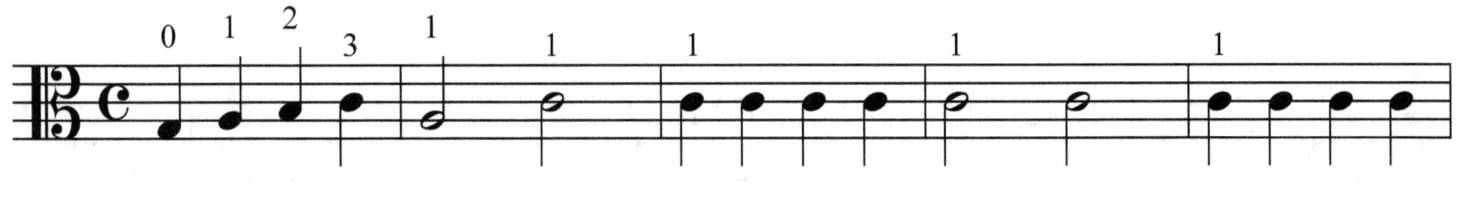

First Shifting on the C string

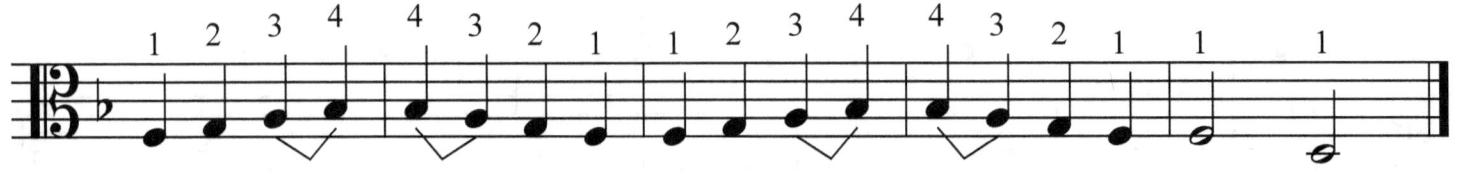

Shifting on the D string

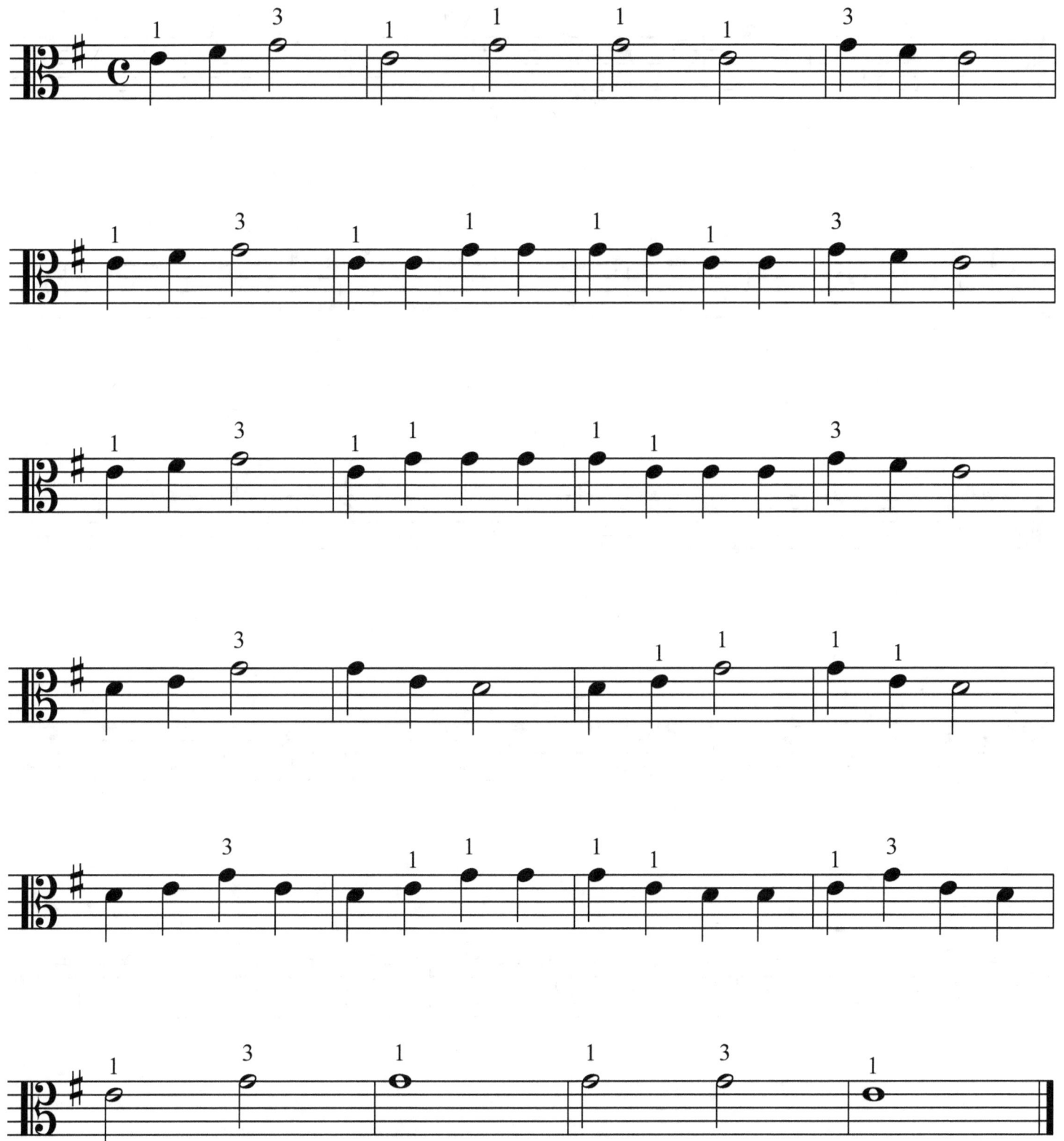

Shifting on the D string and Playing Second Finger A

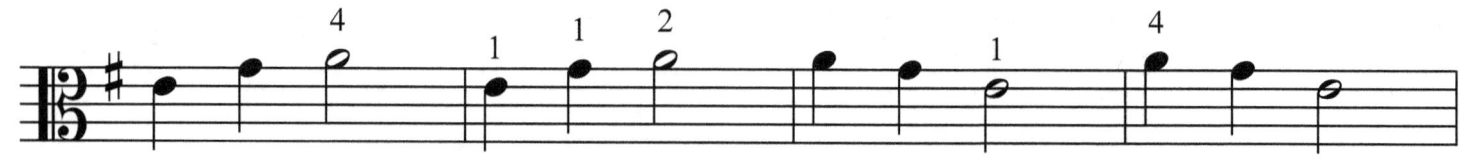

Third Position for the Viola, Book One

Folk Chant

Sea Chanty

©2012 C. Harvey Publications All Rights Reserved.

Shifting on the D string and Playing Third Finger B

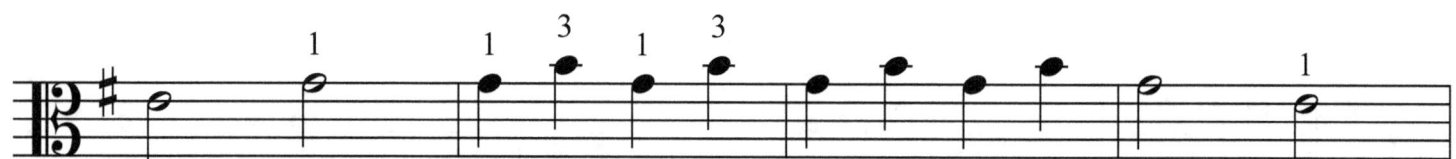

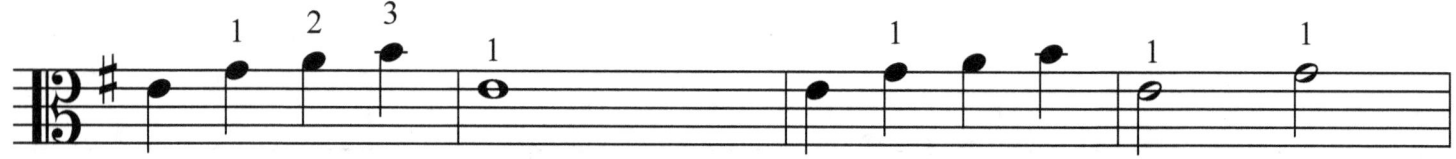

Arkansas Traveler

©2012 C. Harvey Publications All Rights Reserved.

Third Position for the Viola, Book One

Drill, Ye Tarriers

Kansas Traveler

©2012 C. Harvey Publications All Rights Reserved.

Shifting on the D string and Playing Fourth Finger C

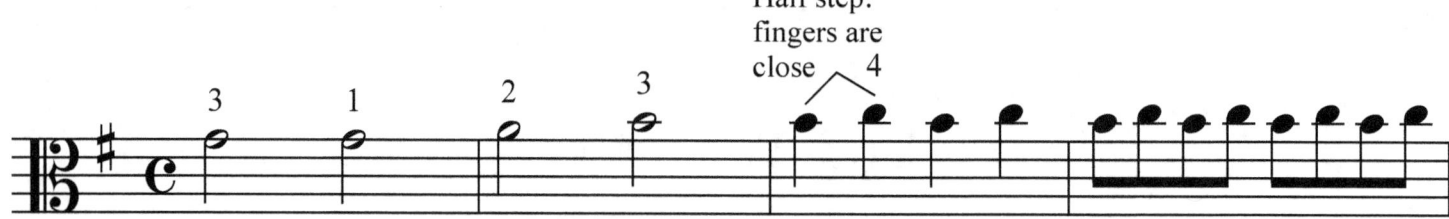

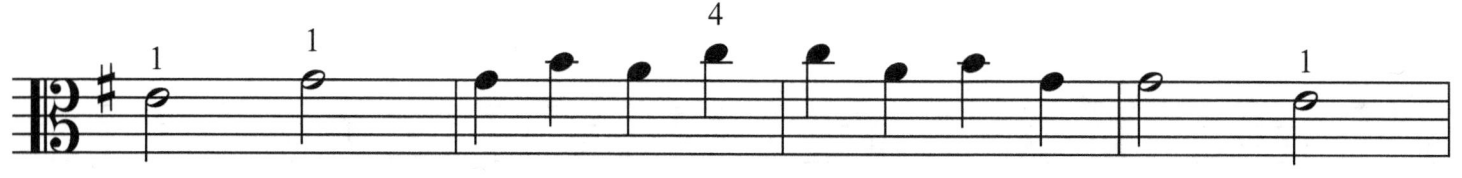

©2012 C. Harvey Publications All Rights Reserved.

Third Position for the Viola, Book One

Shifting on the A string with Slurs

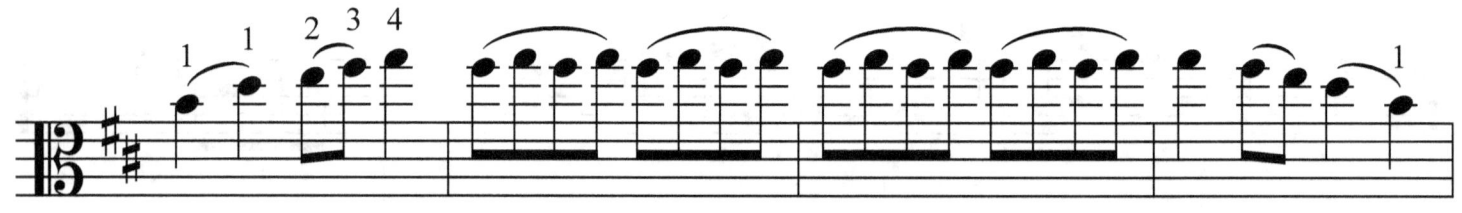

Third Position for the Viola, Book One

Dragons on the River

Starfish Resting

©2012 C. Harvey Publications All Rights Reserved.

More Shifting on the A string

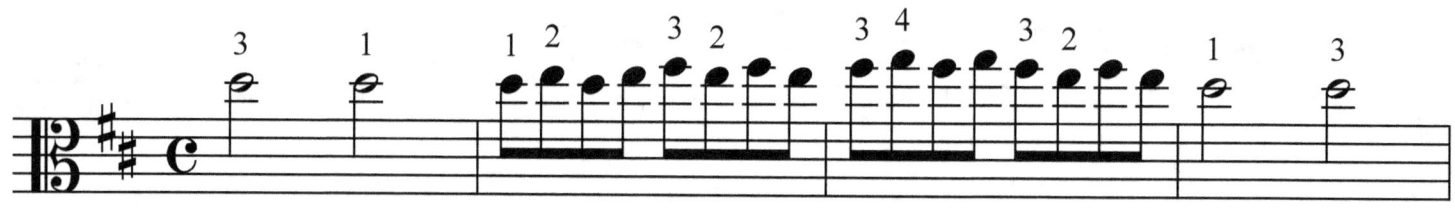

Third Position for the Viola, Book One

Labyrinthine

©2012 C. Harvey Publications All Rights Reserved.

Shifting on the G string

Third Position for the Viola, Book One 15

Warm Sunflowers

Climbing Ivy

©2012 C. Harvey Publications All Rights Reserved.

Shifting on the C string

Third Position for the Viola, Book One

Kudzu

The Velocipede

©2012 C. Harvey Publications All Rights Reserved.

Shifting from 2nd Finger on the D string

Beethoven's Ode to Joy

Spanish Lady: A Traditional Tune

Shifting from 2nd Finger on the A, G, and C strings

Third Position for the Viola, Book One

Paganini's Caprice

Le Couppey's Moderato

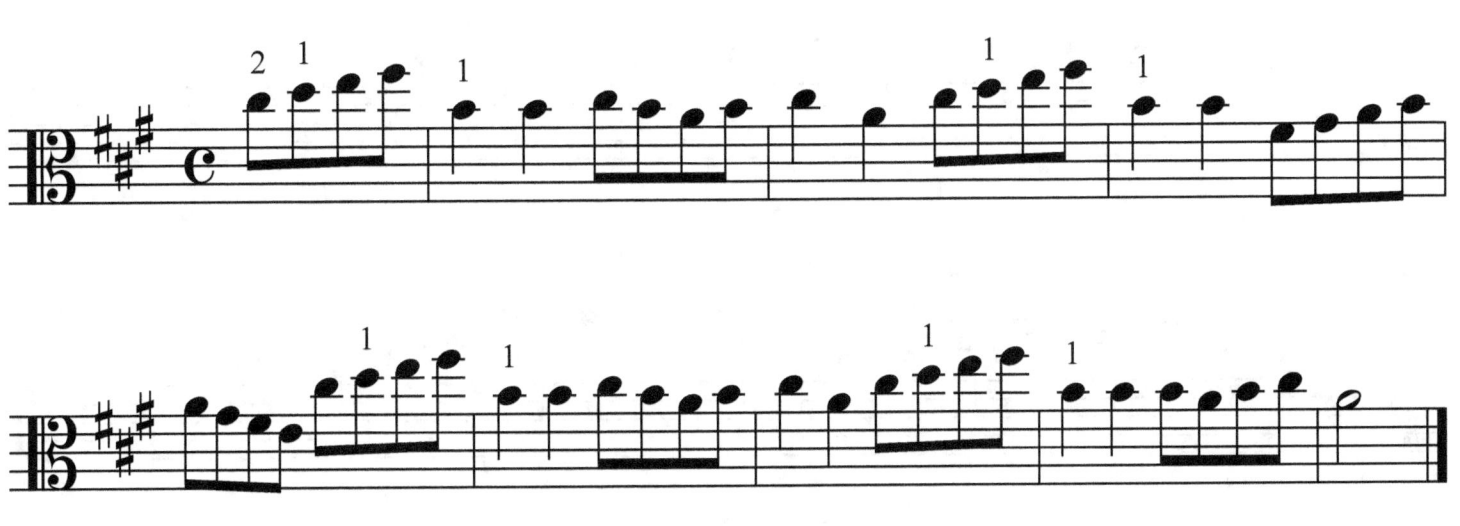

Shifting from 2nd Finger with Slurs

Third Position for the Viola, Book One

Offenbach's Barcarolle

©2012 C. Harvey Publications All Rights Reserved.

Shifting with Slurs

An Anonymous Air

Across Strings with First and Second Fingers

Third Position for the Viola, Book One

27

Martini's Gavotte

©2012 C. Harvey Publications All Rights Reserved.

Across Strings with First, Second, and Third Fingers

Finnish Folk Song

Tchaikovsky's 1812 Overture

She'll be Comin' Round the Mountain

Third Position for the Viola, Book One

Leather Breeches

©2012 C. Harvey Publications All Rights Reserved.

Shifting to and from Second Finger

Fiddle Tune: Cripple Creek

Third Position for the Viola, Book One

G string

Haydn's Surprise Symphony

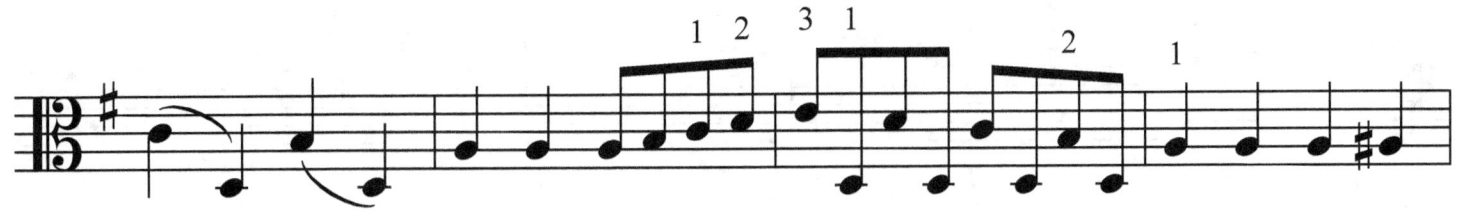

©2012 C. Harvey Publications All Rights Reserved.

Across Strings With all Four Fingers

McMahon's Reel

More Crossing Strings

Third Position for the Viola, Book One

Third Position for the Viola, Book One

The Indian Queen

Star of the County Down

©2012 C. Harvey Publications All Rights Reserved.

Across Strings to Fourth Finger on the D string

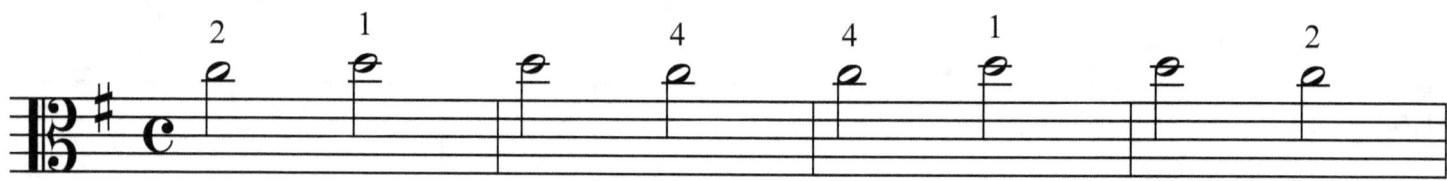

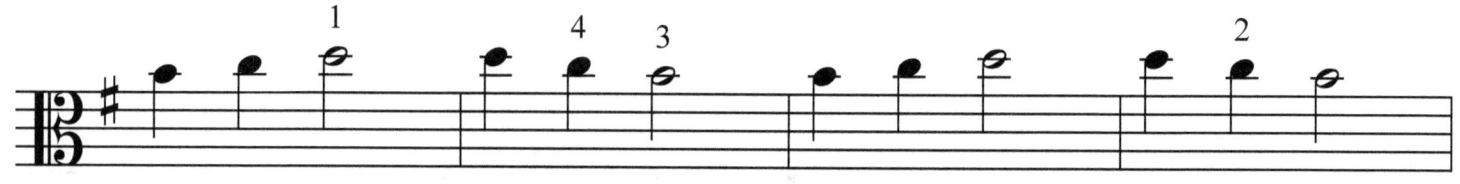

Third Position for the Viola, Book One

Offenbach's Can-Can

Bells

©2012 C. Harvey Publications All Rights Reserved.

Across Strings to Fourth Finger on the G string

Third Position for the Viola, Book One

Buttered Peas

And faster...

©2012 C. Harvey Publications All Rights Reserved.

Across Strings to Fourth Finger on the C string

Third Position for the Viola, Book One 43

Bach's Brandenburg Concerto

©2012 C. Harvey Publications All Rights Reserved.

available from www.charveypublications.com: CHP308

Flying Fiddle Duets for Two Violas, Book Two

The Frog's Courting

Trad., arr. Myanna Harvey

©2016 C. Harvey Publications. All Rights Reserved.

www.ingramcontent.com/pod-product-compliance
Lightning Source LLC
Chambersburg PA
CBHW051426070526
44584CB00023B/3596